Merry Christmas

Erica Fortgens

CANTECLEER

Met veel dank aan de volgende firma's voor geleverde materialen / With many thanks on the following companies for supplying materials / Avec tous mes remerciements aux firmes suivantes pour le matériel fourni / Mit Dank an die folgenden Firmen für gelieferte Materialien:
AVEC, Postbus 678, 5140 AR Waalwijk, tel. (0031) (0)416 567171
Papicolor, Postbus 8010, 3503 RA Utrecht, tel. (0031) (0)30 2433204
Coats Nederland, Brugakker 1025, 3704 KV Zeist, tel. (0031) (0)30 6994469
Fa. Romak, Einsteinstraat 5, 2181 AA Hillegom, tel. (0031) (0)25 20622542

Foto blz.1: beschrijving zie blz. 45 e.v.
Photo page 1: description page 45 and further
Photo page 1: description page 45 et suivante
Foto Seite 1: Beschreibung Seite 45 und weiter

© 2004 Tirion Uitgevers bv, Baarn

ISBN 90 213 3496 8

DTP: Circumflex DTP, Groningen
Photography: Hennie Raaymakers, St. Michielsgestel
Photography styling: Willemien Mommersteeg, St. Michielsgestel
Editor: Loes Brouwer
Translation: Studio Imago, Amersfoort – Cindi Michele Beckman and Anne van der Zwaan
Drawings: Erica Fortgens
Illustrations: Sjaak van Went, Leiden

This book is published by
Uitgeverij Cantecleer
Postbus 309
3740 AH Baarn
The Netherlands

www.tirionuitgevers.nl

Cantecleer is an imprint of Tirion Publishers bv

Voorwoord

Met veel plezier presenteer ik u dit nieuwe boek over borduren op papier. De ontwerpen zijn gemaakt voor de kerst, maar u zult merken dat vele patronen ook heel goed te gebruiken zijn voor allerlei andere gelegenheden zoals een verjaardag, of voor condoleance- en beterschapkaarten. Wanneer u de kleur van de kaart en het garen verandert, krijgt u weer een heel ander effect! Het boek is gemaakt voor de echte borduursters. Ik wens u heel veel plezier.

Erica Fortgens

Foreword

It is with great pleasure that I present you with this new book on embroidery on paper. The designs have holiday themes, but you'll find that many of the patterns lend themselves quite well to many other types of cards (birthday, sympathy or get well cards, for example). Try using a different coloured card and threads for a totally different effect! This book was created for true embroiderers. I wish you much enjoyment and success in your creative endeavours.

Erica Fortgens

Avant-propos

C'est avec un grand plaisir que je vous présente ce nouvel ouvrage de broderies sur papier. Les objets sont conçus pour Noël mais vous constaterez que de nombreux modèles peuvent également être utilisés pour diverses autres circonstances: anniversaire, cartes de condoléances ou de prompt rétablissement. En changeant la couleur de la carte et du fil, vous obtiendrez un tout autre effet. Ce livre est destiné aux véritables amateurs de broderies. Je vous souhaite de longues heures de plaisir.

Erica Fortgens

Vorwort

Mit viel Freude präsentiere ich Ihnen dieses neue Buch über Sticken auf Papier. Die Entwürfe sind für das Weihnachtsfest gedacht, Sie werden jedoch bemerken, dass viele Muster auch sehr gut für allerlei andere Gelegenheiten wie Geburtstag oder für Karten mit Beileidsbezeugung oder Besserungswünschen geeignet sind. Sobald Sie die Farbe der Karte und des Fadens verändern, erhalten Sie wieder einen ganz anderen Effekt! Das Buch ist für echte Stickstars gemacht. Ich wünsche Ihnen sehr viel Freude.

Erica Fortgens

Met veel dank aan / With many thanks to / Avec tous mes remerciements à / Mit Dank an Leonie Heuyerjans, Martha Daniels, Anneke Kaufman, Marijke Hartmans, Sjaak van Went.

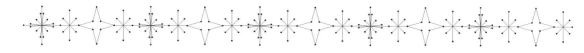

Benodigde materialen

- Prikpen Erica zeer fijn met bijbehorende borduurnaald
- Prikpen Erica fijn met bijbehorende borduurnaald
- Prikpen grof
- Prikmat Erica
- Papier van kaartenkwaliteit
- Plakband
- Lijmautomaat of fotolijm
- Garen Anchor Alcazar Metallic en Anchor Alcazar

Required materials

- Erica extra fine piercing tool with matching embroidery needle
- Erica fine piercing tool with matching embroidery needle
- Coarse piercing tool
- Erica piercing pad
- Card quality paper
- Cello tape
- Glue stick or photographic glue
- Threads: Anchor Alcazar Metallic and Anchor Alcazar

Matériel nécessaire

- Poinçon Erica très fin avec aiguille à broder appropriée
- Poinçon Erica fin avec aiguille à broder appropriée
- Gros poinçon
- Tapis à poinçonner Erica
- Papier à cartes
- Papier collant
- Pistolet à colle ou colle pour photos
- Fils Anchor Alcazar Metallic et Anchor Alcazar

Benötigte materialien

- Prickelstift Erica sehr fein mit dazugehöriger Sticknadel
- Prickelstift Erica fein mit dazugehöriger Sticknadel
- Prickelstift grob
- Prickelunterlage Erica
- Papier in Kartenqualität
- Klebeband
- Klebeautomat oder Fotoklebstoff
- Garn Anchor Alcazar Metallic und Anchor Alcazar

Algemene werkwijze

Prikken

Kopieer het gewenste patroon. Leg het op de kaart, plak het vast met 2 kleine stukjes plakband en leg het geheel op de prikmat. Prik het patroon door de kaart. Gebruik hierbij de zeer fijne prikpen. Voor de gaatjes waar meerdere draden doorheen lopen zijn de prikpennen fijn en grof aan te bevelen. Zorg er in dat geval altijd voor dat het gat groot genoeg is. Houd de kaart tegen het licht om te kijken of alle gaatjes goed geprikt zijn. Het patroon staat nu in de kaart. Verwijder voorzichtig het prikpatroon.

TIP: Houd de prikpen bij het prikken altijd verticaal.

Borduren

Werk stap voor stap volgens de aangegeven werkwijze. Steek bijvoorbeeld achter in bij A, laat de draad achter ongeveer 3 cm hangen en plak de draad achter vast met een heel klein stukje plakband buiten het prikpatroon.

De naald

De naald moet altijd dunner zijn dan de prikpen. Gebruik de borduurnaald uit de verpakking van de prikpen. Als u er moeite mee heeft om de draad door de naald te steken, gebruik dan een draaddoorsteker.

De steelsteek

De toegepaste steelsteek voert u als volgt uit:
1-2 (2-3), 3-4 (4-5),5-6 enzovoorts

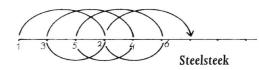

Steelsteek

U slaat bovenlangs altijd twee gaatjes over, onderlangs slaat u één gaatje over. Om een mooie ronding te krijgen borduurt u langs de binnenkant van de ronding, langs de binnenbocht. Mocht een ronding niet goed verlopen, maak dan een steekje extra, het is immers handwerk.

Afwerking

Plak de kaart op een kaart in de kleur van het garen met de lijmautomaat of met fotolijm.

Teksten

Borduur de teksten in steelsteek, trek de draad hierbij niet te strak aan. Soms is het nodig om slechts één gaatje over te slaan.Rand boven aan de pagina: trek draden vanuit het centrum naar de buitenste punten, zo ontstaan sterretjes. Trek de rechte draden van de open ster.

General techniques

Piercing

Make a photocopy the desired pattern. Attach it to the card using two small pieces of cello tape, and then place the card on the piercing pad. Pierce the pattern through the card using the extra fine piercing tool. For the larger holes, I recommend using the fine and coarse piercing tools. At any rate, make sure the hole is large enough for several threads. Hold the card against the light to check whether all the holes have been pierced all the way through. Now carefully remove the piercing pattern.

TIP: Always hold the piercing tool upright when piercing.

Embroidering

Follow the instructions step by step. For example, insert the needle from the back at A, leave around 3 cm of thread hanging, and attach to the back (outside the pattern) using a small piece of cello tape.

Needle

The needle must always be thinner than the piercing tool. It is advisable to use the embroidery needle that comes with the piercing tool. If you have difficulty threading the needle, use a needle threader.

The stem stitch

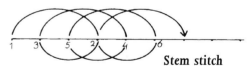

Stem stitch

The stem stitch used for these cards is done as follows:
1-2 (2-3), 3-4 (4-5), 5-6 etc.
Always skip two holes on the front each time and one hole on the back. To create a nicely rounded curve, embroider along the inside bend of the curve. If the curve is not perfectly rounded, simply add another stitch. After all, this is handiwork!

Finishing

Using a glue stick or photographic glue, attach the card to another card that is the same colour as the threads.

Texts

Embroider the texts using the stem stitch. Do not pull the thread tight. You'll need to skip a hole occasionally. Border at the top of the page: Embroider the threads from the middle to the outer dots to create stars. Now embroider the straight threads of the open star.

Methode de travail

Poinçonner

Copiez le modèle souhaité. Posez-le sur la carte, fixez-le fermement avec deux petits morceaux de papier collant et posez l'ensemble sur le tapis à poinçonner. Poinçonnez le modèle à travers la carte. Utilisez le poinçon très fin. Pour les petits trous à travers lesquels doivent passer plusieurs fils, utilisez plutôt le poinçon fin et le gros. En tout état de cause, veillez toujours à ce que le trou soit suffisamment grand. Placez la carte à contre-jour pour vérifier si tous les petits trous sont bien poinçonnés. Le modèle est désormais reporté sur la carte. Enlevez précautionneusement le modèle à poinçonner.

Un conseil : maintenez toujours le poinçon à la verticale lorsque vous poinçonnez.

Broder

Travaillez étape par étape en suivant la procédure indiquée. Piquez par exemple par l'arrière en A, laissez pendre le fil sur environ 3 cm et collez fermement le fil à l'arrière avec un petit morceau de papier collant à l'extérieur du modèle.

L'aiguille

L'aiguille doit toujours être plus fine que le poinçon. Utilisez l'aiguille à broder de l'emballage du poinçon. Si vous avez du mal à passer le fil à travers l'aiguille, utilisez un enfileur.

Le point de tige

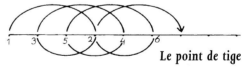

Le point de tige

Le point de tige approprié se réalise de la façon suivante :
1-2 (2-3), 3-4 (4-5), 5-6 etc
Vous passez chaque fois deux petits trous par le haut et un petit trou par le bas. Pour obtenir un bel arrondi, brodez le long du côté intérieur de l'arrondi, le long de la courbe intérieure. Si un arrondi ne se fait pas bien, faites un petit point supplémentaire. Cela reste du fait main !

Finition

Collez la carte sur une carte de la couleur du fil avec le pistolet à colle ou avec la colle pour photos.

Textes

brodez les textes au point de tige, pour ce faire, ne tirez pas trop fort sur le fil. Il est parfois nécessaire de ne passer qu'un seul trou. Le bord supérieur de la page : tirez les fils depuis le centre vers les points les plus extérieurs pour former des étoiles. Tirez les fils droits de l'étoile ouverte.

Allgemeine Arbeitsweise

Prickeln

Kopieren Sie das gewünschte Muster. Legen Sie es auf die Karte, kleben Sie es mit 2 kleinen Stücken Klebeband fest und legen Sie das Ganze auf eine Prickelunterlage. Prickeln Sie das Muster durch die Karte. Verwenden Sie hierbei den sehr feinen Prickelstift. Für die Löcher, durch die mehrere Fäden laufen, sind die Prickelstifte fein und grob zu empfehlen. Sorgen Sie in dem Fall immer dafür, dass das Loch groß genug ist. Halten Sie die Karte gegen das Licht, um zu sehen, ob alle Löcher gut geprickelt wurden. Das Muster befindet sich nun auf der Karte. Entfernen Sie vorsichtig das Prickelmuster.

TIPP: Halten Sie den Prickelstift beim Prickeln immer senkrecht.

Sticken

Arbeiten Sie Schritt für Schritt mit der angegebenen Arbeitsweise. Stechen Sie zum Beispiel hinten bei A ein, lassen Sie den Faden hinten ungefähr 3 cm hängen und kleben Sie den Faden hinten mit einem sehr kleinen Stück Klebeband außerhalb des Prickelmusters fest.

Die Nadel

Die Nadel muss immer dünner sein als der Prickelstift. Verwenden Sie die Sticknadel aus der Verpackung des Prickelstifts. Verwenden Sie, falls Sie Schwierigkeiten damit haben, den Faden in die Nadel einzufädeln, eine Einfädelhilfe.

Der Stielstich

Den angewandten Stielstich führen Sie aus wie folgt:

1-2 (2-3), 3-4 (4-5), 5-6 usw

Stielstich

Überspringen Sie oben entlang immer zwei Löcher, unten entlang überspringen Sie ein Loch. Sticken Sie, um eine schöne Rundung zu erhalten, an der Innenseite der Rundung entlang, entlang der Innenkurve. Machen Sie, falls eine Rundung nicht gut verlaufen sollte, einen zusätzlichen Einstich, es ist schließlich Handarbeit.

Abschluss

Kleben Sie die Karte mit dem Klebeautomat oder mit Fotoklebstoff auf eine Karte in der Farbe des Garns.

Texte

Sticken Sie die Texte mit Stielstich, ziehen Sie den Faden hierbei nicht zu fest an. Manchmal ist es notwendig, nur ein Loch zu überspringen. Rand oben auf der Seite: Ziehen Sie Fäden vom Mittelpunkt aus zu den äußersten Punkten, auf diese Weise entstehen Sterne. Ziehen Sie die geraden Fäden des offenen Sterns.

Kerstfiguren in goud

Benodigdheden

- Papier: Papicolor metallic: 301143 en 301138, Goud: 301102
- Gebruikt garen: Anchor Alcazar Metallic: 9308

A1

Borduur de figuren als volgt: steek achter in bij 1 en trek de draad naar 2. Ga achterlangs naar 3 en trek de draad naar 4. Ga achterlangs naar 5 en trek de draad naar 6. Ga op deze wijze door tot de figuur af is. Cirkels: werk op dezelfde wijze en borduur de cirkel zodanig dat er door elk gaatje 2 draden lopen. Trek de rechte draden van de kerstballen.

Tip: Deze figuren kunt u ook sierprikken. Plak hiervoor het prikpatroon achter op de kaart en prik het patroon door de kaart.

Werk de diverse kaarten af met een strass-steentje.

A1

Christmas figures in gold

Required materials
- Paper: Papicolor metallic: 301143 and 301138, Gold: 301102
- Threads: Anchor Alcazar Metallic: 9308

A1

Embroider the figures as follows: Insert the needle from the back at 1 and pull the thread to 2. Now insert from the back at 3 and pull the thread to 4. Next, insert from the back at 5 and pull the thread to 6. Continue until the figure is complete. Circles: Follow the same method, but embroider the circle using 2 threads for each hole. Embroider the straight threads of the Christmas balls.

A3

Tip: You could also decoratively pierce the figures. To do so, tape the pattern to the back of the card and then pierce the pattern through the card.

Finish off the cards with a strass stone.

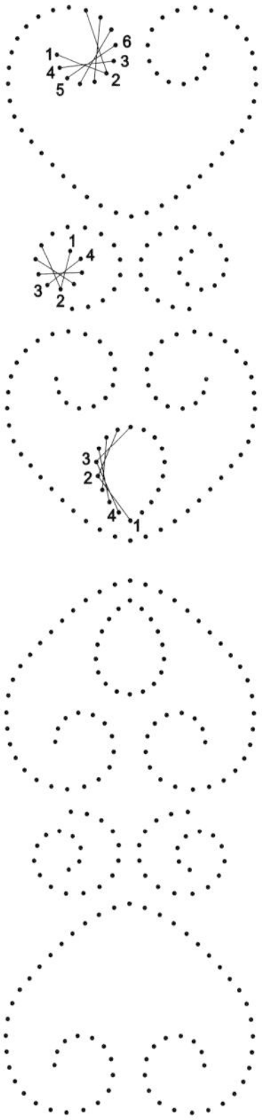

A2

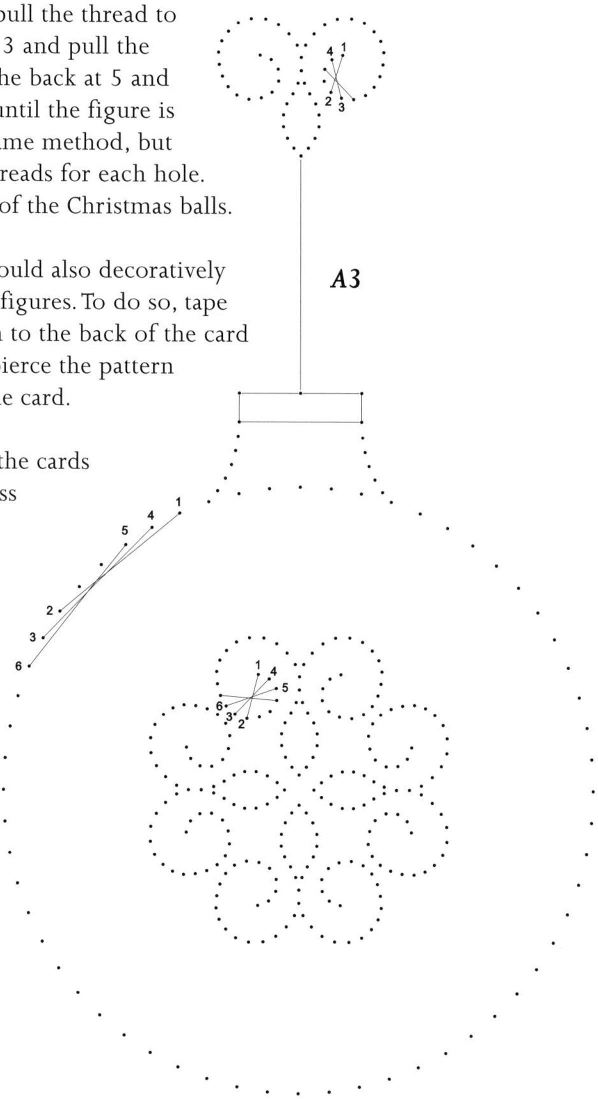

Figurines de Noël en or

Matériel nécessaire

■ Papier : Papicolor metallic 301143 et 301138, Or 301102
■ Fil utilisé : Anchor Alcazar Metallic 9308

A1

Brodez les figurines comme suit : piquez par l'arrière en 1 et tirez le fil vers 2.
Allez par l'arrière vers 3 et tirez le fil vers 4. Allez ensuite par l'arrière vers 5 et
tirez le fil vers 6. Continuez de la même façon jusqu'à ce que la figurine soit
terminée. Cercles : travaillez de la même façon et brodez le cercle de telle sorte
que deux fils passent par chaque trou. Tirez les fils droits des boules de Noël.
Un conseil : vous pouvez également poinçonner les figurines de façon décorative.
Pour ce faire, collez le modèle à poinçonner à l'arrière de la carte et poinçonner le
modèle à travers la carte.

Terminez les diverses cartes avec une touche de strass.

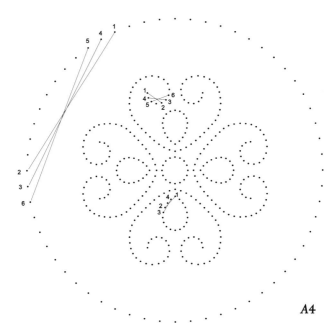

A4

Weihnachtsfiguren in gold

Erforderliches

- ■ Papier: Papicolor metallic: 301143 und 301138, Gold: 301102
- ■ Verwendetes Garn: Anchor Alcazar Metallic: 9308

A1

Sticken Sie die Figuren wie folgt: Stechen Sie hinten bei 1 ein und ziehen Sie den Faden zu 2. Gehen Sie hinten entlang zu 3 und ziehen Sie den Faden zu 4. Gehen Sie hinten entlang zu 5 und ziehen Sie den Faden zu 6. Fahren Sie auf diese Weise fort, bis die Figur abgeschlossen ist. Kreise: Arbeiten Sie auf dieselbe Weise und sticken Sie den Kreis derartig, dass durch jedes Loch 2 Fäden laufen. Ziehen Sie die geraden Fäden von den Christbaumkugeln.

Tipp: Diese Figuren können Sie auch zierprickeln. Kleben Sie hierzu das Prickelmuster hinten auf die Karte und prickeln Sie das Muster durch die Karte.

Schließen Sie die diversen Karten mit einem Strass-Stein ab.

A5

Lichtgroen met roze

Benodigdheden

- Papier: Papicolor 301138
- Gebruikt garen: Coats Reflecta, Alcazar Colour Twist, Anchor Alcazar 9300

B1

Borduur als volgt: steek achter in bij 1 en trek de draad naar 2. Ga achterlangs naar 3 en trek de draad naar 4, enz. Werk de kaart af met een strikje.

B2 en B3

Besjes en blaadjes: steek achter in bij A en trek de draden naar de punten zoals aangegeven. De takjes: worden uitgevoerd in steelsteek. Werk af met kraaltjes en een strass-steentje.

B4

Prik het centrale gat goed groot met de grove prikpen. Steek achter in bij A en trek draden naar de punten zoals aangegeven. Trek de draden van de bloempotten.

Pale green and pink

Required materials

- Paper: Papicolor 301138
- Threads: Coats Reflecta, Alcazar Colour Twist, Anchor Alcazar 9300

B1

J3

B1

Embroider as follows: Insert the needle from the back at 1 and pull the thread to 2, then insert from the back at 3 and then pull the thread to 4, and so on. Finish off the card with a bow.

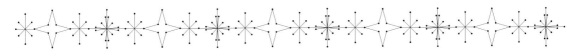

B2 and B3

Berries and leaves: Insert the needle from the back at A and pull the threads to the dots as shown. The twigs are embroidered using the stem stitch. Finish off with beads and a strass stone.

B4

Pierce the centre hole using the coarse piercing pen to make a large hole. Insert the needle from the back at A and pull the threads to the dots as shown. Embroider the threads of the flowerpots.

Vert pâle et rose

Matériel nécessaire

- ■ Papier : Papicolor 301138
- ■ Fils utilisés : Coats Reflecta, Alcazar Colour Twist, Anchor Alcazar 9300

B1

Brodez comme suit : piquez par l'arrière en 1 et tirez le fil vers 2. Allez vers 3 par l'arrière et tirez le fil vers 4. Terminez la carte par un petit nœud.

B2 et B3

Petites baies et petites feuilles : piquez par l'arrière en 1 et tirez les fils vers les points comme indiqué. Les petites branches sont réalisées au point de tige. Terminez avec de petites perles et une touche de strass.

B4

Poinçonnez bien le trou central avec le gros poinçon. Piquez par l'arrière en A et tirez les fils vers les points comme indiqué. Tirez les fils des pots de fleurs.

B2

J2

Hellgrün mit rosa

Erforderliches

- Papier: Papicolor 301138
- Verwendetes Garn: Coats Reflecta, Alcazar Colour Twist, Anchor Alcazar 9300

B3

B1

Sticken Sie wie folgt: Stechen Sie hinten bei 1 ein und ziehen Sie den Faden zu 2. Gehen Sie hinten entlang zu 3 und ziehen Sie den Faden zu 4, und so weiter. Schließen Sie die Karte mit einer Schleife ab.

B2 und B3

Beeren und Blätter: Stechen Sie hinten bei A ein und ziehen Sie die Fäden wie angegeben zu den Punkten. Die Zweige: Werden in Stielstich ausgeführt. Schließen Sie mit Perlen und einem Strass-Stein ab.

B4

Prickeln Sie das mittige Loch mit dem groben Prickelstift groß genug. Stechen Sie hinten bei A ein und ziehen Sie die Fäden wie angegeben zu den Punkten. Ziehen Sie die Fäden von den Blumentöpfen.

B4

J1

Peace

Frohe
Weihnachten

Joyeux
Noel

Kerst in groen

Benodigdheden

- Papier: Papicolor nr. 18 en 43
- Gebruikt garen: Anchor Alcazar Metallic 9308, Alcazar 2: 344

Borduur de figuren als volgt: steek achter in bij 1 en trek de draad naar 2. Ga achterlangs naar 3 en trek de draad naar 4, enz.

C1

Kerstballen: borduur net zo lang door tot er door elk gat twee draden lopen.
Werk af met een strikje.

C2

Borduur de omtrek van het hart in steelsteek.

C3

Kaars: borduren met de steelsteek. Vlam: steek achter in bij A en trek de draden naar de punten zoals aangegeven.

C4

Borduur de omtrek van de boom in steelsteek. U kunt de tekst 'Happy New Year' ook sierprikken. Plak het patroon achter op de kaart en prik de gaatjes door.

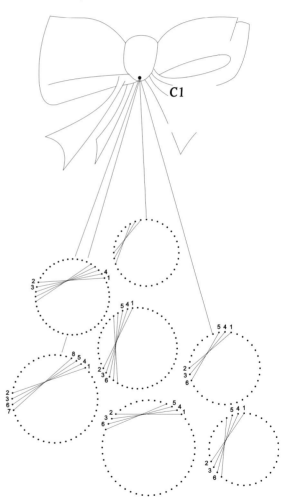

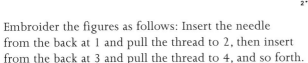

Christmas in green

Required materials

- ■ Paper: Papicolor no. 18 and 43
- ■ Threads: Anchor Alcazar Metallic 9308, Alcazar 2: 344

Embroider the figures as follows: Insert the needle from the back at 1 and pull the thread to 2, then insert from the back at 3 and pull the thread to 4, and so forth.

C1

Christmas balls: Continue embroidering until there are two threads running through each hole. Finish off with a bow.

C2

Embroider the outline of the heart using the stem stitch.

C3

Candle: Embroider using the stem stitch. Flame: Insert the needle from the back at A and pull the threads to the dots as shown.

C4

Embroider the outline of the tree using the stem stitch. You could also decoratively pierce the text 'Happy New Year'. To do so, tape the pattern to the back of the card and pierce the holes all the way through.

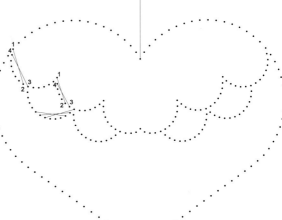

C2

J7

Noël en vert

Matériel utilisé

- ▨ Papier : Papicolor n°18 et n°43
- ▨ Fils utilisés : Anchor Alcazar Metallic 9308, Alcazar 2 : 344

Brodez les figurines comme suit : piquez par l'arrière en 1 et tirez le fil vers 2. Allez par l'arrière en 3 et tirez le fil vers 4, etc.

C1

Boules de Noël : brodez jusqu'au moment où les deux fils passent par chaque trou. Terminez par un petit nœud.

C2

Brodez le pourtour du cœur au point de tige.

C3

Bougies : brodez au point de tige. Flamme : piquez par l'arrière en A et tirez les fils vers les points comme indiqué.

C4

Brodez le pourtour de l'arbre au point de tige. Vous pouvez également poinçonner le texte 'Happy New Year' de façon décorative. Collez le modèle à l'arrière de la carte et poinçonnez les petits trous à travers.

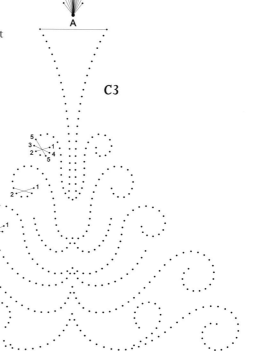

Weihnachten in grün

Erforderliches

- Papier: Papicolor Nr. 18 und 43
- Verwendetes Garn: Anchor Alcazar Metallic 9308, Alcazar 2: 344

Sticken Sie die Figuren wie folgt: Stechen Sie hinten bei 1 ein und ziehen Sie den Faden zu 2. Gehen Sie hinten entlang zu 3 und ziehen Sie den Faden zu 4, und so weiter.

C1

Christbaumkugeln: Sticken Sie gerade so lange, bis durch jedes Loch zwei Fäden laufen. Schließen Sie mit einer Schleife ab.

C2

Sticken Sie den Umriss des Herzens in Stielstich.

C3

Kerze: Sticken mit dem Stielstich.
Flamme: Stechen Sie hinten bei A ein und ziehen Sie die Fäden wie angegeben zu den Punkten.

C4

Sticken Sie den Umriss des Baumes in Stielstich. Sie können den Text 'Happy New Year' auch zierprickeln. Kleben Sie das Muster hinten auf die Karte und prickeln Sie die Löcher durch.

C4

Donkerblauw

D1

Benodigdheden

- Papier: Papicolor nr. 41
- Gebruikt garen: Anchor Alcazar Metallic 9318, 9310, 9311

D1 en D2

Steek achter in bij 1 en trek de draad naar 2. Ga achterlangs naar 3 en trek de draad naar 4. Ga zo door tot de figuur af is. Ovale vormen: borduur net zo lang door tot er door elk gat twee draden lopen.

D3

Trek alle rechte draden van punt naar punt en trek ze stevig aan. Cirkel: zie D1 en D2.

D4

Steek achter in bij de punten A en trek draden naar de punten rondom. Steek achter in bij 1 en trek de draad naar 2. Ga achterlangs naar 3 en trek de draad naar 4, enz. Trek de verticale draden.
Werk de kaarten af met een strass-steentje.

Dark Blue

J5

MERRY CHRISTMAS

Required materials

- Paper: Papicolor nr. 41
- Threads: Anchor Alcazar Metallic 9318, 9310, 9311

D1 and D2

Insert the needle from the back at 1 and pull the thread to 2, then insert from the back at 3 and pull the thread to 4. Continue until the figure is complete. Oval shapes: Continue embroidering until there are two threads running through every hole.

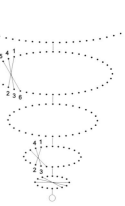

D3

Embroider all straight threads from dot to dot and pull them tight. Circle: see D1 and D2.

D4

Insert the needle from the back at points A and pull the threads to the surrounding dots. Insert from the back at 1 and pull the thread to 2, then insert from the back at 3 and pull the thread to 4, and so on. Embroider all vertical threads. Finish off the card with a strass stone.

D2

Bleu foncé

Matériel nécessaire

- Papier : Papicolor n°41
- Fils utilisés : Anchor Alcazar Metallic 9318, 9310 et 9311

D1 et D2

Piquez par l'arrière en 1 et tirez le fil vers 2. Passez par l'arrière en 3 et tirez le fil vers 4. Poursuivez jusqu'à ce que le modèle soit achevé. Formes ovales : brodez jusqu'au moment où les deux fils passent par chaque trou.

D3

Tirez tous les fils droits, point par point et serrez-les solidement. Cercle : voir D1 et D2.

D4

Piquez par l'arrière aux points A et tirez les fils vers les points autour. Piquez ensuite par l'arrière en 1 et tirez le fil en 2. Passez ensuite en 3 et tirez le fil vers 4, etc. Tirez les fils verticaux. Terminez les cartes avec une touche de strass.

Dunkelblau

Erforderliches

- Papier: Papicolor Nr. 41
- Verwendetes Garn: Anchor Alcazar Metallic 9318, 9310, 9311

Merry Christmas

D1 und D2

Stechen Sie hinten bei 1 ein und ziehen Sie den Faden zu 2. Gehen Sie hinten entlang zu 3 und ziehen Sie den Faden zu 4. Fahren Sie auf diese Weise fort, bis die Figur abgeschlossen ist. Ovale Formen: Sticken Sie gerade so lange, bis durch jedes Loch zwei Fäden laufen.

D3

Ziehen Sie alle geraden Fäden von Punkt zu Punkt und ziehen Sie sie fest an. Kreis: Siehe D1 und D2.

D4

Stechen Sie hinten bei den Punkten A ein und ziehen Sie die Fäden zu den Punkten rundum. Stechen Sie hinten bei 1 ein und ziehen Sie den Faden zu 2. Gehen Sie hinten entlang zu 3 und ziehen Sie den Faden zu 4, und so weiter. Ziehen Sie die senkrechten Fäden. Schließen Sie die Karten mit einem Strass-Stein ab.

D3

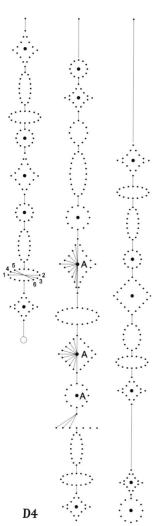

D4

Kerk en engelen

Benodigdheden

- Papier: Papicolor nr. 27 en goud 301102
- Gebruikt garen: Anchor Alcazar Metallic 9300, Alcazar 8: 583

E1

Borduur in steelsteek. Bij de gezichtjes en het haar: een steekje overslaan. Trek de rechte draden.

E2

Borduur in steelsteek. Rand: borduur de hoeken en sierprik de rand. Draai hiervoor de kaart om en prik vanaf de achterkant door de kaart.
Vlammen: steek achter in bij A en trek draden naar de punten zoals aangegeven.

E3 en E4

Borduur de cirkels en de hangornamenten in steelsteek. Trek de rechte draden van de sterren.

E3

Borduur de hulstbladeren, kaarsen en vlammen in steelsteek. Bessen: zie tekening.

E4

Steek achter in bij A en trek draden van de punten van de ster. Maak de boogjes in steelsteek. Borduur de cirkel zoals beschreven bij D1.

E5

Borduur alle gebogen lijnen in steelsteek. Versieringen: sla hierbij slechts één gaatje over. Trek de rechte draden.

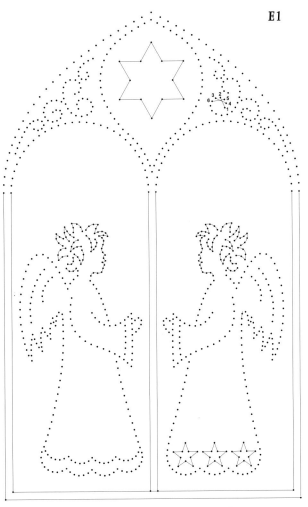

E1

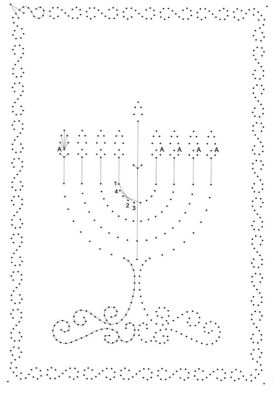

Church and Angels

Required materials
- ■ Paper: Papicolor no. 27 and gold 301102
- ■ Threads: Anchor Alcazar Metallic 9300, Alcazar 8: 583

E1

Embroider using the stem stitch. Skip a stitch when doing the faces and hair. Now embroider the straight threads.

E2

Embroider using the stem stitch. Border: Embroider the corners and decoratively pierce the border. To do so, turn over the card and pierce the holes from the back. Flames: Insert the needle at A and pull the threads to the dots as shown.

E3 and E4

Embroider the circles and hanging ornaments using the stem stitch. Now embroider the straight threads of the stars.

E3

Embroider the holly leaves, candles and flames using the stem stitch. Berries: See drawing.

E4

Insert the needle from the back at A and pull the threads from the points of the star. Embroider the bows using the stem stitch. Embroider the circle as described under D1.

E5

Embroider all curved lines using the stem stitch. Adornments: Skip one hole only. Embroider the straight threads.

E2

Eglise et anges

Matériel nécessaire

- ▨ Papier : Papicolor n°27 et or 301102
- ▨ Fils utilisés : Anchor Alcazar Metallic 9300, Alcazar 8 : 583

E1

Brodez au point de tige. Pour les visages et les cheveux : passez un point. Tirez les fils droits.

E2

Brodez au point de tige. Bord : brodez les coins et poinçonnez de façon décorative le bord. Pour ce faire, retournez la carte et poinçonnez depuis l'arrière de la carte. Flammes : piquez par l'arrière en A et tirez les fils vers les points comme indiqué.

E3 et E4

Brodez les cercles et les ornements à suspendre au point de tige. Tirez les fils droits des étoiles.

E3

Brodez les feuilles de houx, les bougies et les flammes au point de tige. Pour les baies : se reporter au dessin.

E4

Piquez par l'arrière en A et tirez les fils des pointes de l'étoile. Faites de petits arcs au point de tige. Brodez le cercle comme décrit en D1.

E5

Brodez toutes les lignes arquées au point de tige. Décorations : ne passez qu'un seul trou. Tirez les fils droits.

E3

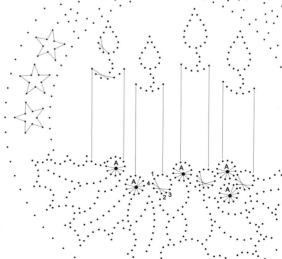

Kirche und Engel

Erforderliches

- Papier: Papicolor Nr. 27 und gold 301102
- Verwendetes Garn: Anchor Alcazar Metallic 9300, Alcazar 8: 583

E1

Sticken Sie mit Stielstich. Bei den Gesichtern und dem Haar: Einen Stich überspringen. Ziehen Sie die geraden Fäden.

E2

Sticken Sie mit Stielstich. Rand: Sticken Sie die Ecken und zierprickeln Sie den Rand. Drehen Sie hierzu die Karte und prickeln Sie von der Rückseite aus durch die Karte.
Flammen: Stechen Sie hinten bei A ein und ziehen Sie die Fäden wie angegeben zu den Punkten.

E3 und E4

Sticken Sie die Kreise und die Hängeornamente mit Stielstich. Ziehen Sie die geraden Fäden von den Sternen.

E3

Sticken Sie die Stechpalmenblätter, Kerzen und Flammen mit Stielstich. Beeren: Siehe Zeichnung.

E4

Stechen Sie hinten bei A ein und ziehen Sie die Fäden zu den Punkten des Sternes. Sticken Sie die Bögen mit Stielstich. Sticken Sie die Kreise wie beschrieben unter D1.

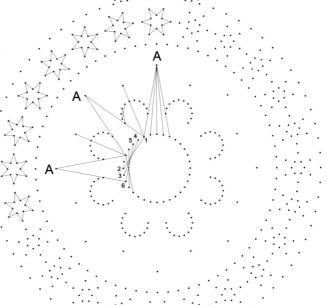

Kruis en kerkramen

Benodigdheden

- Papier: Papicolor nr. 41
- Gebruikt garen: Anchor Alcazar 9326

F1

Gebogen lijnen: bor-duur deze in
steelsteek.
Trek de rechte draden goed aan.
Ronde kerkramen, cirkels: steek achter in
bij 1 en trek de draad naar 2. Ga
achterlangs naar 3 en trek de draad naar
4 enz., tot er door alle gaatjes twee draden lopen.

E5

Sticken Sie alle bogenförmigen Linien mit Stielstich.
Verzierungen: Überspringen Sie hierbei nur ein Loch.
Ziehen Sie die geraden Fäden.

F1

E5

Cross and Church windows

Required materials
- Paper: Papicolor no. 41
- Threads: Anchor Alcazar 9326

F1

Curved lines: Embroider using the stem stitch. Pull the straight threads tight.

Round church windows and circles: Insert the needle from the back at 1 and pull the thread to 2, then insert from the back at 3 and pull the thread to 4, and so on until there are two threads running through each hole.

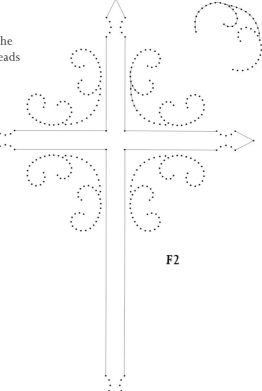

F2

Croix et vitraux

Matériel nécessaire

- Papier : Papicolor n°41
- Fils utilisés : Anchor Alcazar 9326

F1

Lignes arquées : brodez-les au point de tige. Nouez bien les fils droits. Vitraux ronds et cercles : piquez par l'arrière en 1 et tirez le fil vers 2. Passez par l'arrière en 3 et tirez le fil vers 4 etc., jusqu'à ce que deux fils passent dans chaque trou.

F4

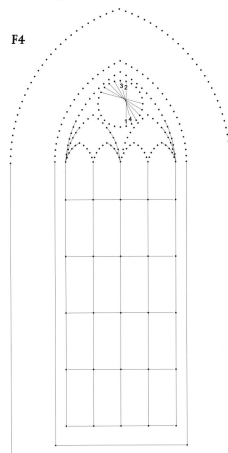

F3

Kreuz und Kirchenfenster

Erforderliches

- Papier: Papicolor Nr. 41
- Verwendetes Garn: Anchor Alcazar 9326

F1

Bogenförmige Linien: Sticken Sie diese mit Stielstich. Ziehen Sie die geraden Fäden fest an.
Runde Kirchenfenster, Kreise: Stechen Sie hinten bei 1 ein und ziehen Sie den Faden zu 2. Gehen Sie hinten entlang zu 3 und ziehen Sie den Faden zu 4, und so weiter, bis durch alle Löcher zwei Fäden laufen.

IJskristallen

Benodigdheden
- Papier: ROMAK mint
- Gebruikt garen: Anchor Alcazar Metallic 9326, 9321

G1

Borduur de boogjes: steek achter in bij 1 en trek de draad naar 2. Ga achterlangs naar 3 en trek de draad naar 4, enz. tot het boogje af is.

G2

Borduur alle cirkels als volgt: steek achter in bij 1 en trek de draad naar 2. Ga achterlangs naar 3 en trek de draad naar 4 enz., tot er door alle gaatjes van de cirkel twee draden lopen. Trek de rechte draden.

G3

U kunt deze figuur borduren (in steelsteek) en sierprikken: in het laatste geval plakt u het prikpatroon aan de achterzijde van de kaart.

G4

Steek achter in bij A en trek draden naar de punten zoals aangegeven. Zorg dat het gat bij A groot genoeg is. Gebruik de grove prikpen.
Trek de rechte draden en borduur de omgeving in steelsteek.

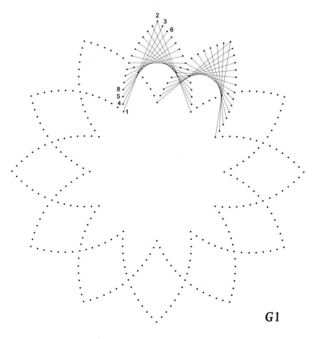

G1

Ice crystals

Required materials
- Paper: ROMAK mint
- Threads: Anchor Alcazar Metallic 9326, 9321

G1

Embroider the curves as follows: Insert the needle from the back at 1 and pull the thread to 2, then insert from the back at 3 and pull the thread to 4. Continue until the curve is complete.

G2

Embroider the circles as follows: Insert the needle from the back at 1 and pull the thread to 2, then insert from the back at 3 and pull the thread to 4. Continue until there are two threads running through every hole in the circle. Now embroider the straight threads.

G2

G3

You can embroider this figure (using the stem stitch) or decoratively pierce it (by taping the piercing pattern to the back of the card).

G4

Insert the needle from the back at A and pull the threads to the dots as shown. Make sure the hole at A is large enough by using the coarse piercing tool to pierce it. Embroider the straight threads. Now embroider the outline using the stem stitch.

Cristaux de glace

Matériel nécessaire

■ Papier : ROMAK menthe
■ Fils utilisés : Anchor Alcazar Metallic 9326, 9321

G1

Brodez les petits arcs : piquez par l'arrière en 1 et tirez le fil vers 2. Passez par l'arrière en 3 et tirez le fil vers 4, etc. jusqu'à ce que l'arc soit terminé.

G2

Brodez tous les cercles de la façon suivante : piquez par l'arrière en 1 et tirez le fil vers 2. Passez par l'arrière en 3 et tirez le fil vers 4 etc. jusqu'à ce que deux fils passent par chaque trou. Tirez les fils droits.

G3

Vous pouvez broder ce modèle (au point de tige) et le poinçonner de façon décorative : dans ce dernier cas, collez le modèle à poinçonner à l'arrière de la carte.

G4

Piquez par l'arrière en A et tirez les fils vers les points comme indiqué. Veillez à ce que le trou en A soit suffisamment grand. Utilisez le gros poinçon. Tirez les fils droits et brodez le cadre au point de tige.

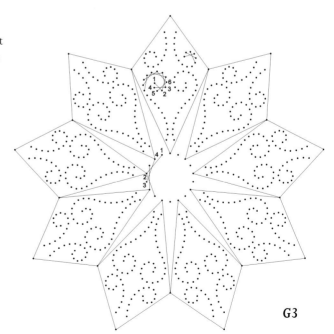

G3

Eiskristalle

Erforderliches

- ▦ Papier: ROMAK mint
- ▦ Verwendetes Garn: Anchor Alcazar Metallic 9326, 9321

G1

Sticken Sie die Bögen: Stechen Sie hinten bei 1 ein und ziehen Sie den Faden zu 2. Gehen Sie hinten entlang zu 3 und ziehen Sie den Faden zu 4, und so weiter, bis der Bogen abgeschlossen ist.

G2

Sticken Sie alle Kreise wie folgt: Stechen Sie hinten bei 1 ein und ziehen Sie den Faden zu 2. Gehen Sie hinten entlang zu 3 und ziehen Sie den Faden zu 4, und so weiter, bis durch alle Löcher des Kreises zwei Fäden laufen. Ziehen Sie die geraden Fäden.

G3

Sie können diese Figur (mit Stielstich) sticken und zierprickeln. Kleben Sie im letzten Fall das Prickelmuster auf die Rückseite der Karte.

G4

Stechen Sie hinten bei A ein und ziehen Sie die Fäden wie angegeben zu den Punkten. Sorgen Sie dafür, dass das Loch bei A groß genug ist. Verwenden Sie den groben Prickelstift. Ziehen Sie die geraden Fäden und sticken Sie die Umgebung mit Stielstich.

G4

Father Christmas

Benodigdheden

- Papier: Papicolor nr. 27 en goud metallic 301102
- Gebruikt garen: Anchor Alcazar Metallic 9300, Alcazar 2: 344, Alcazar 8:555, Alcazar 10:17

H1

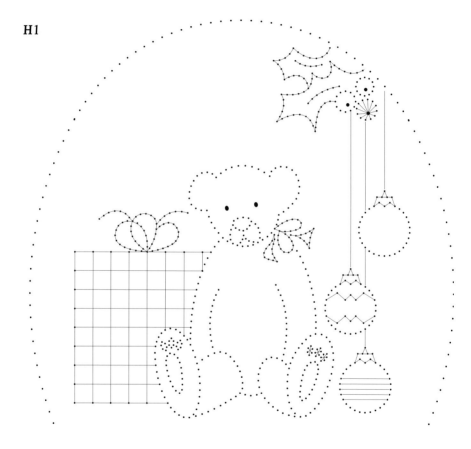

Alle gebogen lijnen worden geborduurd in steelsteek. Bij de fijnere figuren zoals het rendier, de kerstman, de strik van de beer, de vleugels en het haar van het engeltje, slaat u slechts één gaatje over. Trek de rechte draden van punt naar punt.

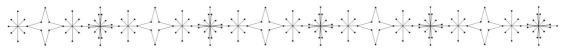

Father Christmas

Required materials
- Paper: Papicolor no. 27 and gold metallic 301102
- Threads: Anchor Alcazar Metallic 9300, Alcazar 2: 344, Alcazar 8:555, Alcazar 10:17

All curved lines are embroidered using the stem stitch. Skip only one hole each time for the finer figures like the reindeer, Father Christmas, bear's bow, wings and angel's hair. Embroider the straight threads from dot to dot.

H2

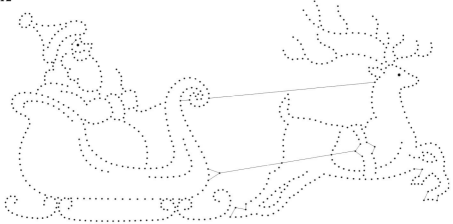

Père Noël

Matériel nécessaire
- Papier : Papicolor n°27 et Metallic or 301102
- Fils utilisés : Anchor Alcazar Metallic 9300, Alcazar 2 : 344, Alcazar 8 : 555, Alcazar 10 : 17

Toutes les lignes arquées sont brodées au point de tige. Pour des figurines plus délicates telles que le renne, le Père Noël, le nœud de l'ours, les ailes et les cheveux de l'ange, ne passez qu'un seul trou. Tirez les fils droits point par point.

Weihnachtsmann

H4

Erforderliches

- Papier: Papicolor Nr. 27 und gold metallic 301102
- Verwendetes Garn: Anchor Alcazar Metallic 9300, Alcazar 2: 344, Alcazar 8:555, Alcazar 10:17

H3

Alle bogenförmigen Linien werden mit Stielstich gestickt. Überspringen Sie bei den feineren Figuren wie dem Rentier, dem Weihnachtsmann, der Schleife des Bären, den Flügeln und dem Haar des Engelchens nur ein Loch. Ziehen Sie die geraden Fäden von Punkt zu Punkt.

Kerstbal en kaarsen

Benodigdheden

- Papier: Papicolor nr. 27
- Gebruikt garen: Anchor Alcazar Colour Twist, Anchor Alcazar Metallic 9300

I1 en I2

Prik de gaten bij A groot met de grove prikpen. Steek achter in bij A en trek draden naar de punten zoals aangegeven.
Borduur bij I1 de figuur af in steelsteek.
Trek bij I2 de rechte draden.

I3

Trek alle rechte draden goed aan.
Vlammen: steek achter in bij A en trek draden naar de punten zoals aangegeven.

I4

Borduur de omtrek van de bal en de onderste en bovenste gebogen lijnen in steelsteek. Andere gebogen lijnen: steek achter in bij 1 en trek de draad naar 2. Ga achterlangs naar 3 en trek de draad naar 4, enz. Werk de kaart af met kralen.

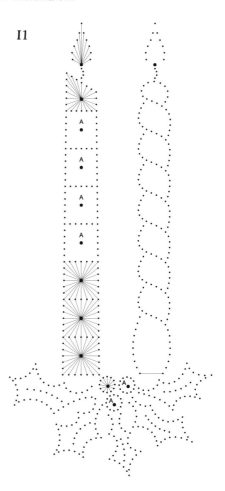

I1

J6

Christmas ball and candles

Required materials
- Paper: Papicolor n. 27
- Threads: Anchor Alcazar Colour Twist, Anchor Alcazar Metallic 9300

I1 and I2

Pierce a large hole at A using the coarse piercing tool. Insert the needle from the back at A and pull the threads to the dots as shown. For I1, complete the figure using the stem stitch. For I2, embroider the straight threads.

I3

Pull all the straight threads tight. Flames: Insert the needle from the back at A and pull the threads to the dots as shown.

I4

Embroider the outline of the ball and the top and bottom curved lines using the stem stitch. Other curved lines: Insert the needle from the back at 1 and pull the thread to 2, then insert from the back at 3 and pull the thread to 4, and so on. Finish off the card with beads.

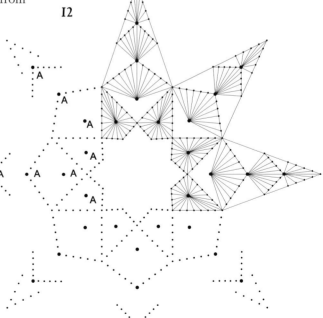

Boule de Noël et bougies

Matériel nécessaire
- ■ Papier : Papicolor n°27
- ■ Fils utilisés : Anchor Alcazar Colour Twist, Anchor Alcazar Metallic 9300

I1 et I2

Poinçonnez les trous en A avec un gros poinçon. Piquez par l'arrière en A et tirez les fils vers les points comme indiqué.
Terminez la figurine en I1 au point de tige. Tirez les fils droits en I2.

I3

Tirez bien tous les fils droits.
Flammes : piquez par l'arrière en A et tirez les fils vers les points comme indiqué.

I4

Brodez le contour de la balle et les lignes arquées du dessus et du dessous au point de tige. Pour les autres lignes arquées : piquez par l'arrière en 1 et tirez le fil vers 2. Passez par l'arrière en 3 et tirez le fil vers 4, etc. Terminez la carte avec des perles.

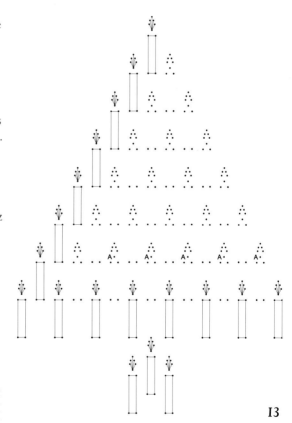

I3

J4

Christbaumkugel und Kerzen

Erforderliches

- Papier: Papicolor Nr. 27
- Verwendetes Garn: Anchor Alcazar Colour Twist, Anchor Alcazar Metallic 9300

I1 und I2

Prickeln Sie die Löcher bei A mit dem groben Prickelstift groß. Stechen Sie hinten bei A ein und ziehen Sie die Fäden wie angegeben zu den Punkten.
Sticken Sie bei I1 die Figur mit Stielstich fertig. Ziehen Sie bei I2 die geraden Fäden.

I3

Ziehen Sie alle geraden Fäden fest an. Flammen: Stechen Sie hinten bei A ein und ziehen Sie die Fäden wie angegeben zu den Punkten.

I4

Sticken Sie den Umriss der Kugel und die untersten und obersten bogenförmigen Linien mit Stielstich. Andere bogenförmige Linien: Stechen Sie hinten bei 1 ein und ziehen Sie den Faden zu 2. Gehen Sie hinten entlang zu 3 und ziehen Sie den Faden zu 4, und so weiter. Schließen Sie die Karte mit Perlen ab.

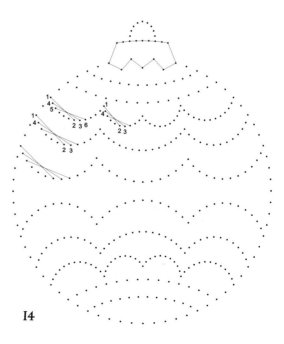

I4